FEB - - 2017

W9-CKW-526

Peabody Institute Library
Peabody, MA 01960

MAGIC CASTLE READERS®

One Tricky Monkey Up On Top

A counting adventure

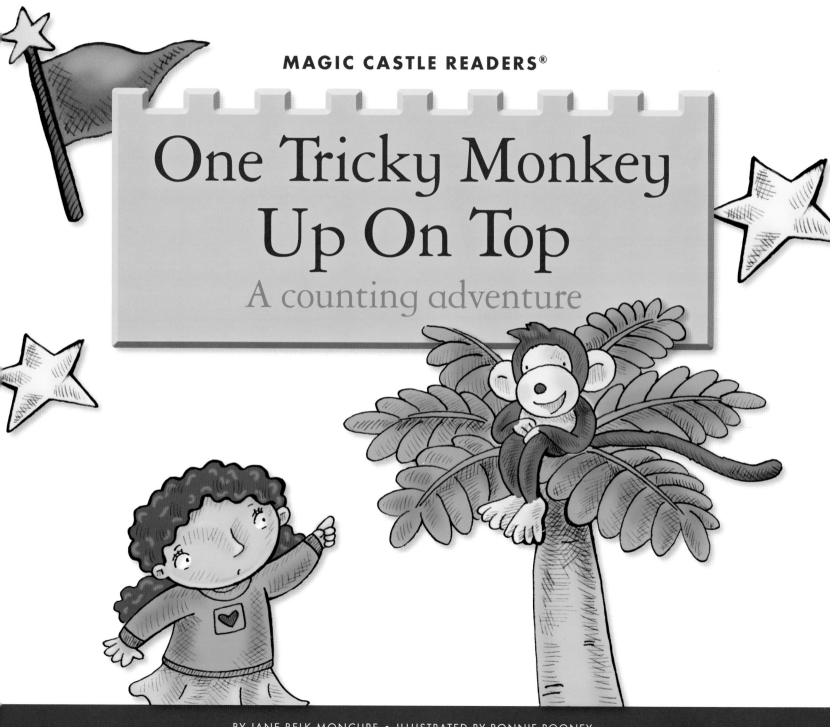

BY JANE BELK MONCURE • ILLUSTRATED BY RONNIE ROONEY

The Child's World®

Published by The Child's World®
1980 Lookout Drive • Mankato, MN 56003-1705
800-599-READ • www.childsworld.com

Acknowledgments
The Child's World®: Mary Berendes, Publishing Director
The Design Lab: Design
Jody Jensen Shaffer: Editing

Copyright © 2014 by The Child's World®
All rights reserved. No part of this book may be
reproduced or utilized in any form or by any means
without written permission from the publisher.

ISBN 9781623235819
LCCN 2013931344

Printed in the United States of America
Mankato, MN
July 2013
PA02177

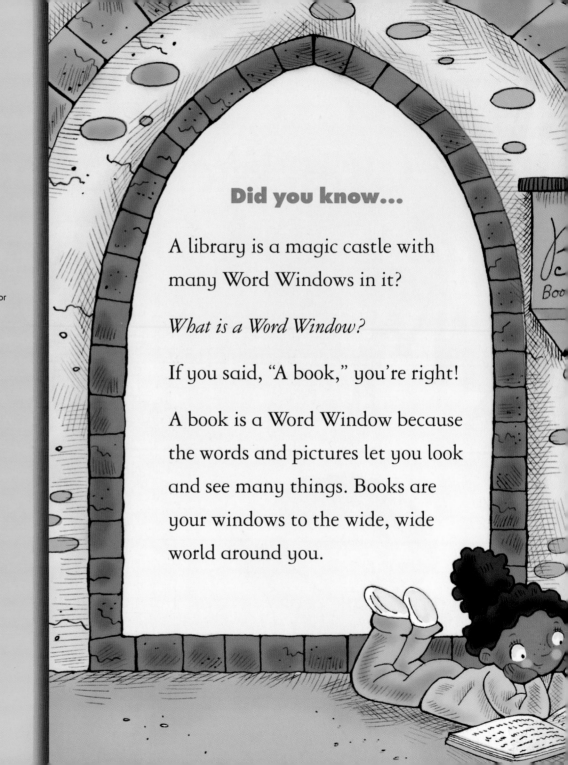

Did you know...

A library is a magic castle with many Word Windows in it?

What is a Word Window?

If you said, "A book," you're right!

A book is a Word Window because the words and pictures let you look and see many things. Books are your windows to the wide, wide world around you.

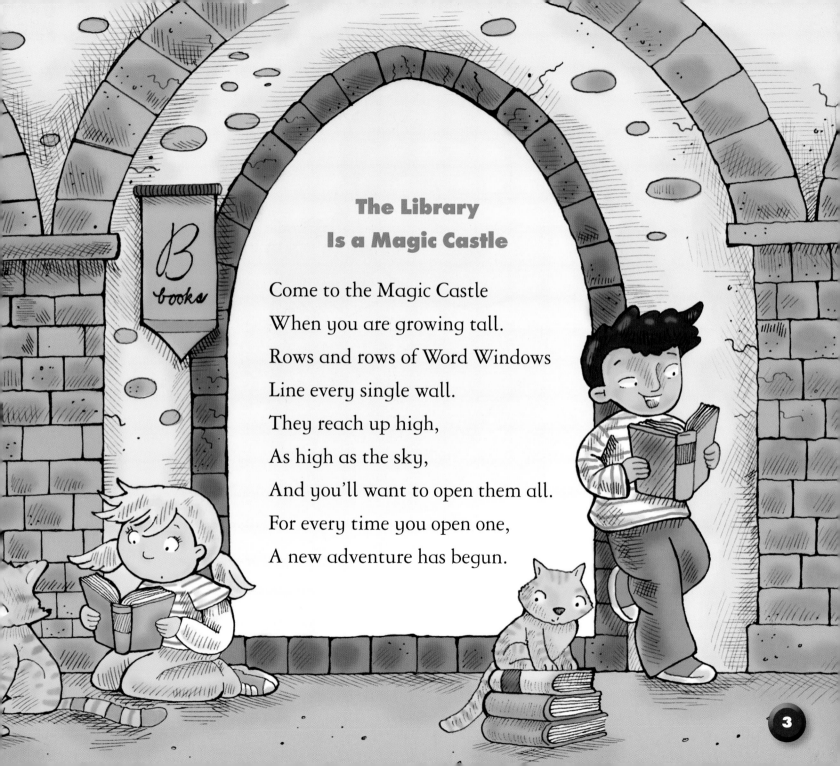

The Library
Is a Magic Castle

Come to the Magic Castle
When you are growing tall.
Rows and rows of Word Windows
Line every single wall.
They reach up high,
As high as the sky,
And you'll want to open them all.
For every time you open one,
A new adventure has begun.

Kara opened a Word Window.
Guess what she saw.

A circus train coming down the track.
Clickety-clack!

"Help," said a little clown.
"My circus animals ran away."

"One tricky monkey went that way."
"I will find him," said Kara.

Kara looked for one tricky monkey on the road.
All she found were hopping toads. How many?

Then Kara looked in a coconut tree.
What did she see?

"Monkey," said Kara. "Come with me."

But Monkey was full of tricks.
He put coconuts on his feet. How many?

Kara put one tricky monkey in car number one.

"Who belongs in car number two?" said Kara.
"Two seals," said the clown.

Kara looked for two seals by the sea.
All she found were fish on a line. How many?

Then Kara looked for seals on some ice.
What did she see?
"Two seals, come with me," said Kara.

She put the seals in car number two.
But what did Tricky Monkey do?
He tickled a seal and made it squeal.

"Who belongs in car number three?" said Kara.
"Three lions," said the clown.
"But I must get the monkey down."

"I will find the lions," said Kara.
She looked for three lions in a truck.
All she found were pigs and a duck. How many?

Then Kara looked for three lions in a box.
All she found were shoes and socks. How many?

Then Kara looked for lions in a cave.
What did she see?
"Three lions, come with me," said Kara.

She put the lions in car number three.
Then Tricky Monkey swooped down from a tree.
He pulled a lion's tail and made it wail!

"Who belongs in car number four?" said Kara.
"Four hippos," said the clown.
Kara said, "Tricky Monkey, you come down!"

Kara looked for hippos in a pen.
All she found were chicks and a hen. How many?

She looked in a pool. What did she see?
"Four hippos, come with me," said Kara.

She put the hippos in car number four.
Guess who crept in through the door.

Who tiptoed on a hippo's nose,
then swooped away on a fire hose?

"Who belongs in car number five?" said Kara.
"Five elephants," said the clown.
  What does Kara say?

Kara looked for five elephants in a house.
All she found were cats and a mouse. How many?

She looked under a banana tree.
What did she see? What did she say?

"Now we can do a trick," said the clown.
"If that Tricky Monkey is still around."

Who is up on top?

Questions and Activities

(Write your answers on a sheet of paper.)

1. How many seals were there in the story?
   How many elephants?
   Add the numbers of seals and elephants. How many do you have?

2. What animal is there the most of?
   How many more of this animal would you need to make ten?

3. Look at the pigs on page 18. Add the number of pigs to the
   number of hippos. How many total pigs and hippos do you have?

4. What does the clown mean when it says the monkey is tricky?
   How do you know the clown means that?

5. Tell this story to a friend. Take only two minutes.
   Which parts did you share?